T0162614

TINNITUS:
A STORM WITHIN

LEARNING THE P.E.A.C.E. STEP

ELIZABETH MARIE KOBE

Inspiring Voices®

Inspiring Voices books may be ordered through booksellers or by contacting:

Inspiring Voices
1663 Liberty Drive
Bloomington, IN 47403
www.inspiringvoices.com
1 (866) 697-5313

Because of the dynamic nature of the Internet, any web addresses or links contained in this book may have changed since publication and may no longer be valid. The views expressed in this work are solely those of the author and do not necessarily reflect the views of the publisher, and the publisher hereby disclaims any responsibility for them.

Any people depicted in stock imagery provided by Thinkstock are models, and such images are being used for illustrative purposes only. Certain stock imagery © Thinkstock.

ISBN: 978-1-4624-1083-5 (sc)
ISBN: 978-1-4624-1084-2 (e)

Library of Congress Control Number: 2014921760

Printed in the United States of America.

Inspiring Voices rev. date: 12/17/2014

CONTENTS

In memory of my Dad, Albert Kobe, who too had tinnitus and sometimes he would say "There goes the tea kettle!" and "Who's whistling at me now?"

INTRODUCTION

"A human being is part of a whole, called by us "universe" a part limited in time and space. He experiences himself, his thoughts and feelings as something separated from the rest a kind of optical delusion of his consciousness. This delusion is a kind of prison for us, restricting us to our personal desires and to affection for a few persons nearest to us. Our task must be to free ourselves from this prison by widening our circle of compassion to embrace all living creatures and the whole of nature in its beauty." Albert Einstein

Tinnitus is like that. It becomes part of one's physical and emotional existence of the world within one's being. The need here is to widen the circle of compassion by understanding others and ourselves as we learn how to comprehend and live with tinnitus while waiting for a cure. As we wait, we can choose to be more constructively powerful than what our thoughts or feelings allow us to do. We can choose to get out of the emotional and physical destructive path of tinnitus storms by forever changing and redirecting negative thoughts and feelings tinnitus produces. Controlling tinnitus is like weathering storms, predictable and unpredictable when dealing with it. When you recognize the unique inner ability of how powerful the brain is in controlling and redirecting the inner noise, consciously or subconsciously the focus on tinnitus stops. Detaching oneself from the tinnitus battle and magnetic attraction it has over the brain takes a real desire to develop coping skills that work.

Having tinnitus makes one live in a unique troubling world of phantom noise. Freeing the self from a tinnitus world can seem impossible. What we choose to do with this world can either bring misery or a life filled with enjoyment. My goal in this book is to inspire you to motivate the will and learn as many alternative ways to put the tinnitus storm to rest forever or at least part of everyday life. To move out of the tinnitus prison walls and learn to enjoy life again to the fullest even if tinnitus remains part of it.

Achieving this success in controlling tinnitus doesn't come easy. Controlling the tinnitus level can have failures or setbacks sometimes, but these setbacks should be a measure in how well you understand your tinnitus and the need to learn skills to control it. Gaining success of control over the tinnitus and acknowledging its' stronghold on the mind will greatly contribute in effectively dealing with it. Tinnitus' best ability is interference in focus and cognitive activities. You can easily lose focus when it is active. You have to practice coping skills to regain this focus and control. In this book, the intervention P.E.A.C.E. Step helped me through difficult moments with tinnitus. Through this experience I learned how words and quotes can be extremely powerful tools in tackling the tinnitus storms. Words can create a diversion that blocks the control tinnitus has over you. Using this P.E.A.C.E step sharpens the skill of mastering control over the inner ear noise. Concentrating on a word or a quote changes the brain's focus when listening to tinnitus. The more I challenged myself with practicing this intervention, the more powerful my control over tinnitus became. Eventually I was able to slow down or stop the tinnitus flare ups quicker. When you begin to understand the physical and emotional operation of tinnitus it will help you grasp better control over the disturbing sound. The P.E.A.C.E method is a great tool of assistance in managing and controlling tinnitus. Take back what tinnitus steals from you and learn the steps to bring back peace.

Acknowledgments

During one of the ATA support group meetings facilitated, many tinnitus sufferers expressed the sounds of hearing peace or silence again. All knew very well how tinnitus robs this silence. Acknowledging this peace loss is a real sense of grief and loss in life by those afflicted with tinnitus. Listening to the feelings of grief and loss produced by the "tinnitus ear" disorder prompted the writings of this book to encourage and help empower other tinnitus sufferers to regain control over tinnitus, to bring back their own sense of peace into their lives once more. Tinnitus grief is a deep feeling that influences the moods and overall wellbeing in how one affectively deals with tinnitus or not. In rediscovering the "Five Stages of Grief"", written by Elizabeth Kubler-Ross, it provided information that helped me connect tinnitus grief and loss to similarities found in this book. With sincere acknowledgement, I am extremely grateful and thankful for her theory and works, and to Mr. Ken Ross, her son, in granting verbal permission to utilize his mother's work. Elizabeth Kubler-Ross's work influenced my ongoing spirit to help others through my book to achieve a positive and

manageable life place with tinnitus. The website www.
ekrfoundation.com is a wonderful and resourceful place to
discover healing.

Many thanks for the years of support to the staff at
the American Tinnitus Association (www.ata.org). Their
support and caring concerns with listening to my numerous
questions, and providing ample verbal information and
literature over the years was a blessing to my tinnitus success.

I am also particularly grateful to my friend Mary
Jellison, of Southwest Harbor, Maine who helped in the
birth of this book by offering her coastal house of solitude
during the cold snowy month of January. There I became
a snowbound hermit waking up to many beautiful Maine
morning sunrises which energized the spirit to continuously
write to nightfall.

Many thanks to Eddie Marencik, whose encouragement
and support made the difference when telling me not to
forget to do the things I love to do when tinnitus was raging.

Thanks to Ken Enhoffer, a tinnitus buddy who not only
assisted in the tinnitus groups but took numerous tinnitus
hikes in all kinds of weather with me.

Thanks to Camille Titone for inspiring confidence.
Thanks to Rosemary Brislin and her "golden ear" in editing.

A million thanks to my brothers Albert and Paul, sisters
Margaret, Kathleen, Jeanne and twin-sister Theresa for
acknowledgement.

Another million thanks to my tinnitus friends who
listened to the conception of the P.E.A.C.E. step to the
final production.

1

POWER OVER TINNITUS

As I was driving home one Saturday afternoon after seeing a movie, I realized there was no ringing in my ears. There was this incredible sense of relief bursting with joy because finally I heard nothing but silence. I didn't bring along this time those protective ear plugs or even attempt to sit in the back seats of the theater away from the sound system. That afternoon of February 9, 2008, I honored this moment of complete silence as a tinnitus survivor because ten years ago after an accidental gunshot triggered the beginnings of right ear tinnitus in 2004, I'd never of thought the possibility of peace ever to return again would occur. In those days tinnitus was ruining my existence.

But life with tinnitus didn't truly stay peaceful for long in 2008. It was compounded again on May 17, 2008 when I experienced a traumatic brain injury after falling eleven feet down off a roof ladder and slamming the left side of the forehead against a concrete cinderblock wall. The impact caused injuring to the auditory nerve and produced tinnitus symptoms in the left ear. Effects from this accident now resulted in bilateral tinnitus; right ear - ringing and left ear - buzzing. Looking back at these triggering tinnitus experiences, I do sense success at conquering control over tinnitus because of the peace I found in living with it. Of course tinnitus is not totally resolved, but I have learned how to regain and master the control over it, learning to let go and live even if it remains a nuisance.

Reflecting on that day in 2004 when tinnitus began, I wondered how I became so successful in controlling it. What coping skills or methods did I utilize? Was it will power and determination to conquer and defeat the "tinnitus" stormy villain? Or was it the freedom of choice to be a survivor and not a victim? Thinking back over the years with how I managed tinnitus, I owe part of this success to the American Tinnitus Association, (ATA). ATA provided plenty of information on what tinnitus is and strategies on how to cope with it. They also received numerous phone calls seeking desperate tinnitus answers from me during difficult moments experienced. With each call made ATA dealt patiently with my venting's of extreme tinnitus frustration, anger, depression, tears and defeat.

In the beginning when tinnitus was taking charge of my life I was scared for my future. I didn't know what to do because of how tinnitus isolated me socially and interfered with work as a nurse. The tinnitus pain made me scream and complain constantly. Often the idea of jumping out of a window came to mind because of the unbelievable tinnitus loudness and pain. It was so immobilizing. Whatever I did to stop the crazy ringing wasn't working. Being emotionally miserable, the joy of life was truly slipping away. Was this disorder ever going to resolve itself? Am I going to have to live with this forever? It was not until one long phone call conversation with a supportive and empathetic ATA staff that I realized something has to change. The change needed was not the angry negative attitude harbored against tinnitus, but me. I needed to change.

After recognizing I was the stumbling block towards a positive tinnitus turnaround, the effects of the raging tinnitus over me began to eventually diminish. Since I was handling the hearing disorder negatively, tinnitus was defeating me at the ability to control the levels of noise. I needed to change this negative attitude to a positive one in how I approached and dealt with the tinnitus problem. Instead of constantly engaging in the downward spiraling negative thoughts I became more optimistic in coping and regaining noise control. An attitude adjustment was surely needed.

Having the mindset of tinnitus becoming worse fed this negative attitude. The fear gave tinnitus permission to stay in the forefront of controlling thoughts. I neglected the responsibility to take charge in changing the negative thinking which was a detriment in moving forward to any healthy change. As I surrendered my will to tinnitus, the noise remained a constant. Looking back at the onset of tinnitus, the negative outlook was also compounded by a statement from the ENT doctor, "There is nothing you can do about it, just live with it". This defeating thought dissolved my overall power to control tinnitus. The power in this defeating statement inadvertently changed my will instantly making me submissive to the tinnitus control.

Unfortunately, the first deterrent some people combat with on the road to tinnitus recovery is the attitude of the initial diagnosing doctor. As mentioned above, the negative thought "nothing you can do about it" is quite a destructive statement when trying to recover. How often is this heard by newly diagnosed sufferers? Doctors send you home with a negative attitude without any coping idea on how to live with it. Though they might suggest and prescribed medication for it. But, is this the only tool for the tinnitus solution, medicine? Isn't there any coping skill or information the doctor could provide other than say "go home and live with it"? Isn't there a place or person who can provide help and understanding? There is no reason for anyone to feel a lack of support or abandonment when diagnosed. All of these tinnitus questions have answers. There are many resources of information to provide them.

As mentioned above, my desperation for help was needed. When I made that morning phone call to ATA, I understood that part of the solution to tinnitus was engaging a positive mind to it, but what were the other parts to the solution. One other part was me and the other missing part was found in a single word an ATA staff member mentioned in that phone call conversation in which I wrapped my mind around it. This one particular word was "control". It hit me like a ton of bricks and stilled my thoughts because I didn't have the control necessary to control tinnitus. The solution to tinnitus is to take back the control.

Learning how to take back the control was the vital solution to my emotional and physical wellness. The tinnitus havoc interfered in many areas of life. The desperation of wanting a normal life without noise had to be accepted by changing the emotional attitude towards life with noise. To stop and begin coping with the crippling noise that was affecting my wellbeing. I discovered I had to somehow retrain the brain to control it. Hearing that word control, helped to change the defeating negative mindset and not let the disturbing sounds control me. There was only one conscious decision for a tinnitus sufferer to make was to start saying "NO" to tinnitus and "YES" to life. The first method in controlling tinnitus is by saying no. No more living in the negative. To change the direction of how the noise interferes.

Changing the attitude to take control taught me how to live with tinnitus successfully. The feelings of loss and abandonment from tinnitus can stop from existing. Tinnitus has no ownership in your ability to control, it's not destructive, it's just a hearing disorder.

Coming to Experiencing Tinnitus

As you have come to experience tinnitus, it is a perception of sound when no external sound is present. Which literally means the sound is only in your head and nowhere else. It is a phantom sound heard with no external origin. According to ATA pamphlet, "Understanding Tinnitus", it is often described as "ringing in the ears and varies tremendously from person to person. Some people hear roaring, buzzing, high pitch tones similar to emergency broadcast signals. Some hear only one sound, while others several." Some hear train wheels braking, or a dull tapping, or a high pitched ringing in the key of E.

Whatever sound (s) you hear, whether it is constant or intermittent, severe or not so severe, it's presence is individually well known and felt. Tinnitus has a raging nature; it can suddenly appear and can suddenly disappear. No one can predict the onsets or disappearance of tinnitus since it has a unique nature. Overall, tinnitus does not have to be the same sound to everyone though similar in distraction. It can be debilitating to some and not to others. How tinnitus started matters somewhat, but how you decide to deal with it, matters the most. The decision here rests on your choice to be positive or negative when learning how to deal with it. How you manage to live with it is solely up to you as well as the amount of determination you have to control it. Being negative by using self-defeating words like, "I can't", only gives the tinnitus more control. The choice to challenge control and utilizing positive words, like "I can" aids you in conquering the troublesome tinnitus. It is all according to your willingness to change.

Since the cure for tinnitus hasn't been discovered and still being researched, how one develops a solution for their own tinnitus is by use of a coping skill or device that helps the present condition. Even your inborn ability to change the negative tinnitus course can be the manageable working cure or solution. The cure to tinnitus starts with you. Start exploring which solution or device helps bring relief. The solutions or skills utilized to change the tinnitus nature will alter how it interferes in your life. Sometimes, you have to stop, pause, and look at any negative influence that impairs your ability to successfully cope with the disorder. Are you negative or positive about wanting help? Do you easily give up on solutions? Do you spend time reinforcing coping skills? As you become more aware of how tinnitus negatively affects your life, finding remedies to ease the affliction will be the positive reinforcement. Remaining positive builds reinforcing qualities and skills that help gain total ability in controlling tinnitus.

Trying to Survive

As a survivor, tinnitus flare-ups can suddenly happen and impair the ability to focus. Flare-ups create problems in school, employment, hobbies, and anything that requires focus. While being employed in the medical field, tinnitus greatly disturbed and distracted my ability to accurately listen to heartbeats of patients when using a stethoscope. The annoyance of ringing made me miscalculate heartbeats, interrupting focus. Trying to refocus on the heartbeat was often difficult due to the interference of tinnitus sounds. Because I was in a vital position regarding patient heart care, I had to quickly learn how to ignore the tinnitus flare-ups and refocus on my job. Handling these flare-ups developed into the P.E.A.C.E step. When I lost focus, I would take off the stethoscope and think of a word like "stop" and repeat it several times until I began refocusing. It took plenty of practice working with this intervention to refocus and quieting the tinnitus. Tinnitus distractions eventually became easier to handle.

In the last chapter of this book, P.E.A.C.E, you will find how words and inspiring quotes help support you to cope, control, and conquer tinnitus by teaching you how to distract it. Each day as you practice this method, it will become a significant powerful tool in lessening the interference of tinnitus magnetism. When you redirect tinnitus your control improves and life gets better.

2

EMOTIONAL AND PHYSICAL

Unfortunately, tinnitus effects a person's emotions and physical wellbeing. It lowers the tolerance for patience and creates anxiety. It disrupts our happiness and peace in countless ways. Probably you are at the point of frustration dealing with the tinnitus and looking for help. When you picked this book up, it was a positive testimony that you want relief from the constant struggle and suffering of tinnitus. That tinnitus is adversely affecting you both emotionally and physically. The depression, lack of peace, anxiety and anger is causing a silent pain that you don't think anyone is aware of your suffering. It interferes in almost everything you do as in sleeping, concentration, what to eat or what not to eat, social and physical activities, work, etc. Perhaps some days, you barely get out of bed or just hide in your house because of the way you feel. The darkest of days that were imagined are here. Self-pity or commiserating about the effects of tinnitus is a huge emotional problem. "Why me"?

Often when the mindset is like this, you lose touch with living for the moment. Instead, rather than taking charge and challenging the control over tinnitus, you let the abundance of negative feelings create an unforgiving environment of dismay. Since tinnitus resides in the emotional limbic section of the brain, the phantom noise creates a roller coaster of unsettled feelings. Tinnitus does produce negative emotions that can easily pull you away from enjoying life. This depressing drowning effect tinnitus has is a common problem among sufferers in regards to emotional tinnitus pain and often goes misunderstood.

The drama of a tinnitus crisis or storm can become life's focal point. You can't stand in the center of the emotional tinnitus storm without any use of a coping skill. The dynamics and strength of the tinnitus complexity can eventually take a toll on your health, both emotionally and physically. Tinnitus can be cyclic. Emotions can be cyclic. Both create havoc and offset balance of wellbeing. Even though tinnitus is an ear disorder, it doesn't mean to create a self-pity or self-defeating behavior in one's health. There are two words that can change the emotional nature of a tinnitus crisis or storm within. They are *can* or *can't*. Saying *I can*, is powerful in defeating the storm. Saying *I can't*, is as powerful and sustains the life of a storm. It is your choice of control, either you *can* or *can't* change tinnitus power over you.

Another two words are either you *will* or you *won't*. Either you will walk towards change or you won't walk towards change. Deciding the direction of the storms outcome is which words you choose. Will you or won't you, can you or can't you decide if you have the self-winning attitude that makes you the master over tinnitus?

Medical research shows that tinnitus resides in the emotional area of the brain and therefore explains the reason why tinnitus affects a person's emotional balance as in stress, anxiety, moods, and happiness. Having control over our tinnitus emotions is influenced by what choices are made that will effectively deal positively with the emotional and tinnitus brain. The emotional areas along with the disturbances of tinnitus sounds does affect thinking and often people challenged with this problem become frustrated, have issues with anxiety and can feel depression. In the brain the tinnitus causes hyperactivity that interferes with cognition and focus for a sustained period of time. With this occurring daily, the compounding negative emotional tinnitus thoughts defeat and breaks down good innate coping skills of control. It affects the healthy balance of the emotional limbic brain. The least one does in changing the course of a negative tinnitus influence, the more opportunities tinnitus has to keep you emotionally unbalanced. Any loss of emotional control adds to a depressive state as well as to other areas of health.

Understanding the effects of the undesirable mechanics of tinnitus gives more reason to learn how to control it. The hyperactivity tinnitus produces in the brain does affect sleep according to ATA. Therefore a tinnitus brain is never at rest. If the brain does not get adequate rest, the body, mind and ability to function daily will be affected. This is one of the reasons why it is important to develop a skill to help control and slow tinnitus down since it is so active in the brain.

Helping one-self emotionally by investing personal time and practice with alternative coping interventions can bring back levels of wellness. There are many treatments and or therapies suggested by ATA such as cognitive therapy, biofeedback, drug therapy, self-help books. Sound therapy, as according to Better Hearing Institute says "that the presence of background sound reduces the prominence or loudness of tinnitus. Music can also be very effective in quieting the tinnitus by non-wearable and wearable devices. Wearable devices are maskers or sound generators that produce an encouraging noise that blankets the tinnitus sound. Non-wearable devices can be headphones or playing the stereo, radio, television to hear an alternative sound to mask the tinnitus sound." Music played at a safe level brings calmness while masking the tinnitus.

Tinnitus can also affect the physical aspect of the body. Over indulgence with foods can be a comfort measure but it's an unhealthy coping skill. Food is only a temporarily relief and increase consumptions of certain foods like coffee/tea (caffeine), chocolate, salt, alcohol and preservatives can increase the levels of noise, worsening tinnitus. It also increases blood pressure and can trigger a flare-up. According to Dr. Theodore Herazy article "Tinnitus Self-Help", February 5, 2008 in www.Article Alley.com, he states "anyone who has had tinnitus for a few years knows what aggravates the problem. Make a point of view of anything known that increase the problem, such as being around tobacco smoke, drinking alcohol, and any loud noise will accentuate the tinnitus."

Since self-help books provide keys or skills in gaining self-control over tinnitus, it is your responsibility to find the right key(s) or skill(s) that unleashes tinnitus control and sets you free. ATA website is a key that provides information on gaining control as to a healthy diet. The auditory nerve needs to be protected and preserved for good hearing and prevention of tinnitus crisis. Vitamins such as B's provide healthier nerve repair and processing. Eventually you will discover what foods, vitamins, medications, activities and stressors help or worsen your tinnitus. Tinnitus recovery always involves an increase in physical activities such as walking or any exercising that increases the levels of good endorphins. Exercise lowers the levels of anxiety, creating better feelings about self. It also helps your brain from focusing on tinnitus. Also, talking with a nutritionist can be part of your recovery too. Whatever you learn will help maintain a healthier and manageable tinnitus. Start moving away from the ills of tinnitus and learn how to influence your tinnitus health positively.

3

THE POLLUTION – TOXIC THINKING

Toxic thinking can also affect emotions and physical wellbeing. Toxic thoughts can impair motivation and the power within to change the negative tinnitus forefront. At times when one experiences the unwelcomed internal noises, unfavorable unpleasant feelings are produced such as anxiety. The noise in the head is so amplified that toxic thoughts can take over the whole self. "Why did I get this, I don't deserve to suffer!" "I will never enjoy life again, it is so unbearable!" Rather than being positive about the disability, there are moments one becomes downhearted and depressed. Emerging thoughts appear gloomy and pessimistic which can downwardly shift wellness to an unhealthy disposition. The negative mind focused on tinnitus remains on an irritable edge, toxic to wellbeing. This is tinnitus toxic pollution.

Toxic attitudes shows up in our thoughts often as "I am so worn down, I don't feel like doing anything", "I can't live with this anymore, it's killing me" or "If I have to live with this noise forever, it will drive me insane", "I don't feel like doing anything anymore", "No one really cares about this noise in my head", "I don't care how I am, this noise is bothering me and I want the world to know it." The obsessiveness and constant rumination of such thoughts chews away at the healthy mind. It begins to wither the physical body by interrupting sleep causing fatigue. Alienation from social activities, friends, and family becomes increasingly noticeable. Whatever hobbies or activities you enjoyed in the past becomes less of an interest. For example, perhaps you have decided not to go dancing or to a musical show because of the loud music or talk knowing that it will bother the tinnitus level. You start making excuses and fear activities you once enjoyed. Toxic tinnitus thinking has become part of your everyday personality and prevents you from living an active happier life. It lingers around like a gloomy gray cloud reminding you how awful having tinnitus is. Because tinnitus generates a hyper negative sound, how one effectively deals with it is entirely up to the temperament of your attitude. The tinnitus is in your head or ear, but it doesn't reside in the whole self. It doesn't control your interests in life. You control your interests. Of course, tinnitus can mentally challenge you from the initial date of onset, but learning how to deal effectively with it does lessen the toxicity. Confront your motivation to change the unhealthy environment to a better being. How one reacts to the tinnitus also indicates how effective your coping skills are towards betterment. Is your emotional brain still attached to the effects of tinnitus? Remember, even though as irritating tinnitus is, the part of you that influences the negativity alters mental and physical balance. You need to constantly work at detaching the mind from any onset of toxic tinnitus thoughts since it can affect the whole body balance. If you are experiencing unfavorable thinking, then this is the time for change.

Through the studies of biological science, it reveals the anatomy and physiology of a human body to be comprised of various tissues, arteries, blood, organs, nerves, extremities, and other parts that make it operate successfully. When diagnosed with tinnitus, the peaceful smooth operation of hearing is interrupted by damage in the cochlea, the inner portion of the hearing organ. The damaged in this area introduces unwanted noise. The phantom sound heard is now part of the human ear functioning. The constant tinnitus sound flows around the way blood does. Because of this phantom sound the emotional part of our brain somehow stays emotionally connected to it. It becomes part of memory. Phantom sound is memory from former noise heard. This unwanted sound creates a disturbance that afflicts the body. Without taking control over tinnitus sounds, it becomes venomous to the smooth operation of the whole body. This hearing disorder can hinder you in all areas of life, from proper nutrition, exercise, output of work, socialness. By letting this disorder create imbalances, it will definitely wither and change the outlook of your life. Does it have to? Why let it persist? Why let it spoil wellness and leave you living in phantom pain?

Whatever physical and mental power relinquished to tinnitus will only produce unhealthy consequences. Deterioration in wellbeing begins with lack of control. As you continue to unhealthily attach the whole body to tinnitus, the power relinquished eventually damages the wellness environment. It will adversely work its way into family, friends, and possibly career. Tinnitus becomes part of your day to day personality and possibly brings out the worst in you as in moments of anger and depression. Whatever behavior you have allowed with tinnitus has created a change in a good balance. The toxic tinnitus is running life.

Having this negative toxic attitude should be the decision maker to change your tinnitus environment. Remaining negative produces negative attention. As life continues to persist with toxic thoughts, then self-pity becomes your crutch. If you continue to permit these toxic thought crises, then your brain will have a harder time dealing with change and self-control. Remember pessimism is an obsessive toxin to the brain because it conditions you to do nothing.

Problems in Support

When toxic pessimistic tinnitus thoughts exist in a person's presence, it becomes increasingly difficult for supportive people to interact with them. Supporters that aid a tinnitus person who does little in finding self-help tire. If a tinnitus sufferer continues to interact with others in a toxic way, the environment tends to withdraw and perhaps perceive them as a failure. When a toxic tinnitus sufferer says, "My family never understands me." or "No one is helping me.", they are transferring blame to helpful supporters. Eventually the supporter's optimistic contribution is felt unwelcomed, inadequate and devalued. Concerned people begin to distant themselves and eventual support dissolves. No one wants to be your tinnitus crutch. Because you feel the world doesn't understand your tinnitus hardship, it doesn't mean to show it like an open wound. Remember keeping emotionally attached to tinnitus is harmful to all relationships. As you find help, the environment surrounding you will interact favorably and will want to be a source of help. By making tinnitus toxicity less, the disorder becomes manageable. Strive to be an activist in coping positively, utilize skills that change tinnitus' ongoing ability to interrupt peace. Find healthier steps to control tinnitus. Start reaching for peace and get rid of the toxicity.

4

STAGES

In the early weeks of my tinnitus, I often felt depressed and hopes of it going away were very dim. Tinnitus wasn't disappearing as fast as it came. The tinnitus sounds produced were quicker than any high speed internet. Peace was replaced with a constant irritating screeching noise. The battle with tinnitus persisted daily. Friends and family said, "Not to worry about it. It will eventually go away". After months of waiting for it to resolve, people would say "You still have it!" Tinnitus wasn't resolving on its own, nor was I resolving it. There was no quietness in my head or within my constitution. Weeks of devastating tinnitus turned into unending months of endless struggling. Intervals of constant screeching train wheels, endless dull tapping, and high pitched "Eeeeeeee"'s haunted my ears with pain. Was it here to stay forever? Life felt impossible then. Tinnitus, the dark phantom of noise in my head shadowed days of restlessness. It bore an interior prison sentence with no defining crime committed. Peace was diminishing and I wanted this peace back. But the question remained, how?

After the phone call (mentioned in Chapter 1) with the ATA staff, I worked hard at maintaining the positive attitude and control required to deal with the ongoing tinnitus. To help me understand this condition and deal with it effectively, I began exploring other avenues of information which provided alternative coping skills such as ear maskers, headphones, ear plugs, hypnosis treatments, counseling, diet and the significance of reaching out to other tinnitus people for support. Since tinnitus made me feel isolated, I needed to begin socializing with people who were also affected by tinnitus. With ATA's guidance, I facilitated a monthly local support group that would be a source of help to others with this ear disorder. Conversing with other tinnitus people alleviated the isolation felt and provided relationships to safely vent with. After a few group meetings, there was one topic prevalent in all of the discussions; the need for peace inside the head, as well as interior peace. This perpetual quest for one peaceful moment was a goal for many. The attendees would complain of not having a day of no sounds in their head for a very long time as well as what peace would sound like again. Some thought this type of peaceful silence wouldn't be recognized because of the time loss knowing it. The constant activity of tinnitus sounds retrained the normal brain to think tinnitus sound is the sound of peace, but it is an abnormal peace. If tinnitus ever became silent, would normal peace be acknowledged? Would it be known to the sufferer? To some sufferers it would be like a miracle to experience, but of course, only with a fear of tinnitus returning.

During the support group meetings people shared concerns on how tinnitus interfered with daily activities. The distraction, lack of focus, and cognitive thinking were constant problems. One group member, Anthony, who suffered with tinnitus for over 15 years, reported uninterrupted daily sounds of a penetrating jack hammer. That presently no solution has helped him. He stopped talking to doctors and seeking alternative help. But recently in the local newspaper, he saw the ad about the tinnitus group and thought it might help him. When meeting him for the first time, his affect was negative and depressed. A group member offered a helpful idea in dealing with tinnitus and Anthony negatively refused the idea of listening to music to mask the tinnitus. He made himself and tinnitus unapproachable. He reported that for years he stopped complying with medical advice on medication, exercise program, diet and wearing of protective earplugs in his construction job. Anthony said "The doctor doesn't have it, so how can he help? He doesn't understand my suffering at all." Since this was the first supportive group he came to, he had difficulty of letting go of his displaced tinnitus anger. His deteriorating attitude battled with the uplifting positive group support. Eventually, as he listened to others, it became his first step towards changing the negative attitude harbored. He began to emotionally open up and stated feelings of how similar his issues were to the members. How tinnitus pain defeated and wore him emotional down dismantling his personal relationships. His quest for a tinnitus free life seemed impossible.

Although it was Anthony's free choice to remain negative about the disorder by not taking proactive measures in changing the control or moving forward to learn how to, he remained a tinnitus victim. His negative choices increased depression, thereby altering peace. Though he continued to meet with the group, the comfort and support provided by others eventually helped him to gain insight to change his tinnitus world regaining control and obtaining interior peace.

After meeting Anthony and learning about his tinnitus life, I realized I was like him in the past. Anyone who is affected by tinnitus and presently not working to control it can experience a depression similar to his because of the loss of silence and peace within. The search for happiness and peace is easily lost because tinnitus somehow attacks the interior will to be positive. The interior calmness gives way to tinnitus anxiety. By surrendering control to tinnitus it allows it to create opportunity for emotional unbalance. Allowing tinnitus to claim victory over your peaceful life, the anguish and unbalanced emotions continues to imprison you. Relinquishing to this position, tinnitus is victorious over both interior and inner ear peace.

In exploring the pain of tinnitus sufferers there is a deep desire for the return of this inner and ear peace. But how does one return to these types of peace? Before any coping skill can be successful to this return, one has to process the loss of a dying peace. The perfect sense of hearing peace has been damaged or destroyed. This dying of peace is recognized by the amount of grief and depression associated to it. The first step towards dealing with these issues is to find a coping method to alleviate the grief and depression. Since psychological and emotional issues are involved, any lack of acceptance and positive change towards these issues keeps the tinnitus in control negatively. The state of depression grows.

Acknowledging how difficult my own tinnitus was, these negative effects of tinnitus made me become more aware of learning how to discharge these numerous unwanted feelings. It took various coping skills and much effort to stop focusing on the loss and difficulties in order to bring back a sense of peace. Though there were many rough times in coping and competing with tinnitus control, I often found myself falling backwards into being a victim of grief again. As like Anthony, I too had not initiated a proactive behavior at the onset tinnitus. Becoming positively proactive with good coping methods like earplugs, hypnosis, support groups and skills that developed self-control, my peace returned. I felt freedom as the tinnitus grief and loss dissolved.

Five Stages Recognized

When I was employed in the medical profession, I often discussed the "Five Stages of Grief" by Elisabeth Kubler-Ross, to patients suffering significant tragedies with emotional and physical loss. These losses ranged from significant death, surgical removal of body parts or organs, mental illness, diseases, cancers, separations, divorces, addictions, miscarriages, accidents, or any other life changes severe enough that's considered a loss and where pain emerges from. With all tragedies there is some form of grief in loss observed. Since tinnitus can be a tragic change for many, it can also be a tragic loss that alters life dramatically. Tinnitus can be a debilitating disorder and comes with feelings of undesired emotions: crying, anger, sadness, grief and etc. Examining this well of negative tinnitus emotions how does one process it? How does one cope and regain balance in life? How does one stop the worrisome thoughts of a worsening tinnitus? Will peace ever be attainable? Will depression ever leave? Will this fear of lost peace forever cloud the anxious mind? Answers appear impossible. What blocks the success in gaining peace and control over the loss tinnitus produces? Can an individual choose to stop these obstacles and bring peace back by another means? Yes one can by simply do this by accepting it.

In the five stages of grief as Elisabeth Kubler-Ross explains in her book, "Death and Dying", there are five words that express the stages of grief: denial, anger, bargaining, depression and acceptance. In each stage listed below there are comments I have heard from tinnitus sufferers that you might feel familiar with.

Stage 1   **Denial/Isolation** – "This cannot be happening to me now." "I can't believe this incredible noise!" "No one else is experiencing this, nobody understands it!" syndrome.

Stage 2   **Anger** – "How could this happen to me? What did I do?" "It isn't fair." "I wish you had it!" Tinnitus sufferers often project emotional and physical anger, rage, envy at self and others.

Stage 3   **Bargaining** – "I'll say a few prayers for peace in my head". "I need a miracle?" Maybe you begin to think that doing a good deed, stopping a habit of some kind, even negotiating with the higher power to change the level of tinnitus.

Stage 4   **Depression** – "I give up". "I feel like jumping off a bridge." "Who really cares about me?" "I am all alone with this." One might be alienating from social activities, remaining in bed, missing days at work, maybe even crying more often over the tinnitus dread, convinced there is no hope.

Stage 5   **Acceptance** – "I can't keep living like this; I need to accept and move on with my life." "I have to work with it." "I have to change." This is when positive decisions are made to change the direction of the tinnitus darkness and get back into the mainstream of life. The "I can" do it attitude.

The Need to Accept

Most tinnitus sufferers can agree they might be stuck in one or two of the stages listed or experienced all of them and finally accepted tinnitus. Some say at the onset of diagnosis they accepted tinnitus without experiencing another stage. But some sufferers who don't experience acceptance right away bounce back and forth between stages. How can you get to this acceptance stage and deal with tinnitus having a sense of balance of peace inside? Again, as mentioned before, the only way to acceptance is by accepting tinnitus. That is the only realistic choice towards healing and control. Since tinnitus at times can be a cyclic non- stop noise, the difficulty in keeping this balance of peace is due to your ability to control the influences of tinnitus. Acceptance is when one chooses to change the negative influences of tinnitus. Emotional balance seeks a positive will in the need to accept life with tinnitus. Accepting it increases tolerance towards it, thereby more control over it. Tinnitus behavior becomes easier to understand and live with. Understanding how tinnitus fires up negative emotions, one then can put out the fire. Any positive proactive choice alters the tinnitus attitude and changes the course of recovery. The healing begins.

Recognizing Fear of Self-loss

Digging deeper into my tinnitus reflection, it appeared that being stuck in these cycles of tinnitus grief produces another sense of greater loss. That greater loss is losing oneself to it. Any failure to progress through these 5 stages listed above was primarily due to the negative defeating attitude that a mind engages in, thereby causing self to spiral downwards in depression. This fear of total loss becomes the deconstructive catapult that alters the mind from moving forward and out of the depression of having tinnitus. As fear buries itself in the memory cells of the brain it changes the positive will into a negative one. But this fear can also be a trigger that alarms the self to stop the cycle of ups and downs in emotional behavior by recognizing this continuing loss of self is unwanted. When the pain of losing self becomes unbearable, it becomes the obvious time to change the tinnitus course of destruction. The tinnitus personality can't linger anymore when a choice to change is made. Strongly build up the mind with unyielding confidence and determination with positive coping skills altering the undesirable consequences of tinnitus.

In these five words and stages: denial, anger, bargaining, depression and acceptance, the tinnitus sufferer has to understand the transformation of this tinnitus grief. That experiencing the stage of grief is a progression towards healing and self. As you come to accept tinnitus as a part of life you can move forward. If you find yourself stuck in any stage, obtain help to prevent stepping backwards into grief and depression. Any progressive and positive efforts will bring you closer to the goal of living peacefully with tinnitus. Develop good coping strategies and keep a tinnitus storm at bay.

5

TAKING BACK OWNERSHIP OF CONTROL

Taking back your ownership of controlling tinnitus can either be simple or difficult to achieve because of the personal challenges one faces when learning how to deal it. The will must be able to take back full charge of control and never allow tinnitus to take over again. Taking control over the impulsive and intrusive noises starts with recognizing this lack of control one has over tinnitus. Because a tinnitus mind has a magnetic embrace over your mindset or presence, learning how to distract the compulsive tinnitus mind might be the hardest part in taking back ownership of control. If you can imagine the power of a magnet, then you can how imagine powerful tinnitus is with the mind. As the mind is easily distracted by the compelling tinnitus noise; concentration and focus is also influenced. Concentration and focus is necessary in performing daily living activities. Tinnitus's ability to disturb concentration illustrates a lack of mind control over the intrusive noise. Any type of inner ear noise distracts focus, thereby produces a stressor of anxiety in concentration. The stress changes to fear of tinnitus worsening and ability to focus. This powerful fear of tinnitus effects eventually weakens your will and trying to control tinnitus seems impossible. Remember while tinnitus affects focus and concentration it also disturbs emotions. Taking back ownership of control is being responsible in moving forward. In doing so, the chances of tinnitus influencing your moods, emotions and thoughts will change for the better. By empowering self-control over tinnitus, tinnitus loses its ability to irritate life. By not redirecting your self-control over the pain, you're relinquishing control back to tinnitus. It becomes cyclic and tinnitus problems continue to escalate due to your lack in ownership.

Now how do you take back ownership of control if you are always under the influence of tinnitus control? How is your behavior responding? Are you triggered emotionally becoming short-tempered? Do you have some control? There must be some reasons why you can't take back full ownership of control. In the book, "How to Get What You Want and Want What You Have", written by John Gray, Ph.D., it addresses success and obtaining it. "Become aware of the twelve common blocks that could be holding you back from having what you want and begin to clear the way for both inner and outer success. Learn to release any of the twelve blocks that may be holding you back: blame, depression, anxiety, indifference, judgment, indecision, procrastination, perfectionism, resentment, self-pity, confusion and guilt." [1] As being a tinnitus sufferer success can be hindered by any one of those blocks mentioned in trying to obtain control over tinnitus. Try figuring out which block or blocks are preventing you from moving forward. By discovering which block hinders success in controlling tinnitus, you can then unblock it by accepting the block(s) or problem(s) and engage in a coping skill to change the ownership of control. Do you know which one of the block(s) is controlling your tinnitus? Be proactive and unlock the block (s).

As you begin to unlock the blocks there is a change in the level of negativism that decreases as the level of optimism grows. The emotional brain is becoming better equipped in handling control over tinnitus. This growth of optimism reinforces the ego to take charge over tinnitus difficulties. Whenever tinnitus pain is felt, the brain can quickly look at the reactions blocking control. When this occurs make notes and observations so that when something triggers tinnitus you can quickly unlock the blocks that are hindering control of it and the affects. Building up on a variety of coping skills will greatly improve control over the interrupting and raging sounds quicker. It will lessen the possibilities of slipping backwards out of control creating

---

[1]   How to Get What You Want and Want What You Have. John Gray. New York: Harper Collins Publ., 1999, p. 4

more blocks to peace. Take charge of life; be positive and confident that you can change your tinnitus's destiny and outcome by discovering what the problems are. Be in control of your tinnitus life.

6

THE P.E.A.C.E. STEP

To help in supporting tinnitus control and the stages mentioned in Chapter 4, I developed a coping method for control called the P.E.A.C.E. Step. It is a simple self-help method or skill to learn and can be implemented at anytime, anywhere to help from falling backwards into the stages of grief and loss and when tinnitus erupts or disrupts harmony. It will also help you gain control with focusing and concentration. The main goal in this P.E.A.C.E Step is to teach you how to use your innate power of the brain to tackle the tinnitus stormy flare-ups. In the P.E.A.C.E Step each letter stands for words of authority reminding you who's in control. Each letter and word represents you as the powerful step towards recovering interior and exterior peace.

You are the power within the P.E.A.C.E. Step:

P   power and persistence

E   embrace and endurance

A   action and adjusting

C   challenge and conquer

E   enjoyment of life

In Chapters 7 and 8, each letter of P.E.A.C.E. illustrates how words and quotes can be a wonderful and challenging tactic in controlling tinnitus storms. It is a defensive method against tinnitus. As this method becomes a daily coping skill in dealing with tinnitus distractions, it will help you to become calmer and more in control when tinnitus brews. This method or technique requires your brain to practice harder at being attentive when focusing on words or quotes to control the activity of sounds produced. Each letter in P.E.A.C.E is a continuous working step towards the ability to stop tinnitus interferences. Understand there is power in words and word power can influence control over tinnitus. The P.E.A.C.E. step leads you to this control and success.

7

MEANING OF
P.E.A.C.E. LETTERS

P = Power – Persistence

Innate power changes the direction of will because it is the determination in oneself to do so. You need both power and persistence to change the controlled area of the tinnitus brain where it controls the emotional you. Despite the difficulties and the problems that exist with tinnitus, the amount of brain power you allow determines how it will alter the problems and difficulties of the mesmerizing tinnitus. Willpower determines this course of recovery.

Many sufferers falter with control at the onset of tinnitus because of not understanding how to use the power of the mind to change it from within. Perhaps due to low esteem and loss of an in-charge personality, one allows tinnitus to rule over the will. Or it could be from stating, "I can't do this anymore" or "I give up!" indicating a loss of control power within. Maybe you can't deal with tinnitus at the moment, but try to understand that any negative thought is influenced by you and can be replaced by your innate positive power to change this direction of thought. Being empowered is to silence tinnitus by ignoring it and retrieving control. Of course it takes effort and time to ignore and redirect the tinnitus but it can be done. Be active, be persistent and take control of your recovery. Transform the powerful effects of tinnitus by transforming your control. Persist by being assertive with change. Have hope, belief and work at it with coping skills no matter how bad tinnitus becomes. As Franklin D. Roosevelt once said, "When you come to the end of your rope, tie a knot and hang on." Now that's real power. Defeat tinnitus by using the power from your mind. Now think, do you have the power and persistence to defeat tinnitus? Will you be the winner of the tinnitus struggle?

E = Embrace – Endure

It is easier to embrace people, animals or beauty when there is no pain, but when pain exists it is not so easy. So, how does one embrace and endure the painful emotional and physical effects of tinnitus? When you start to accept tinnitus, you begin to embrace and endure it. The core in endurance and embracing tinnitus is the courage to face its' pain and learn how to adapt. Unfortunately tinnitus is a part of your life and living side by side with it takes patience and tolerance. As you embrace it with understanding and acceptance you undergo a transformation in attitude towards it. You begin to move forward in freeing yourself of any difficult attachments to the painful feelings of it. Know that as you seek the pathway to tinnitus freedom, joy will return. There is no need for tinnitus to destroy the joy in life. Keep saying, "I am okay, it is only tinnitus." "I am okay, it is only tinnitus."

In embracing tinnitus one has to befriend it as if it was like a talkative person, who can't be quiet. If this person telephoned you might say, "it's not a good day" or "I am too busy to talk." You choose not to make time for them. How you deal with this type of person is the same way you deal with tinnitus noise. When the tinnitus flares up like a talkative friend, talk to the tinnitus like you would talk to this friend. Embrace the moment by mentally or verbally saying words to quiet it down, "go away, I am not paying attention to you right now". Talking to the tinnitus can limit the tinnitus potential effects. Since tinnitus is a miserable intruder, building a relationship with it by saying, "okay, I know you are here, you can leave now" can actually alter or redirect tinnitus to a quieter level. Basically, you are instructing tinnitus to do what you want it to do by influencing it by words of command. The conscious brain working with positive commanding word power will control flare ups. Whenever flares up occur, try to redirect it by saying, "be quiet, be still, be quiet, be still" until the noise level lessens. Remember, tinnitus is a trial of working patience. As you learn to embrace and endure tinnitus, you will have more control over it.

A = Action – Adjusting

When you decide to take the necessary actions to adjust to life with tinnitus, this will be the enlightened moment in dealing with the difficulties. The responsibility in taking action is to adapt and work alongside of tinnitus changing the negative to positive. You have chosen to step away from the controlling nature of tinnitus by allowing the tinnitus to exist by adapting to the nature of it. This doesn't mean you're letting tinnitus run your life, it's the exact opposite, you are allowing it as part of who you are now. As you learn to adjust, the success of control over annoying sounds greatly improves.

The effort that is required in action is to find what coping skills work best. When tinnitus becomes a disturbance, take some form of action that adjusts your reactions to the sounds. Individual effort is crucial in how you affectively deal with tinnitus noise. By concentrating and working with effective coping skills daily, tinnitus will become increasingly manageable. The willingness to discipline the self in tinnitus thought control takes commitment in changing the role tinnitus engages you in. You are not a servant to it. As you adapt to a tinnitus life any step or action that changes control sets your mind apart from listening to the tinnitus. This is a step in conquering the distraction. For example, if you're in a noisy restaurant inform the waiter of the possibility of a flare up or how sensitive tinnitus is and ask for a quieter area. In advocating your tinnitus voice you're taking action by being in charge. Adapting to change will help you deal more effectively with unpleasant tinnitus moments out in the real world. It becomes easier to deal with the internal anxiety because you're in charge.

Understand that noisy people and environments can be a precipitating factor in producing heightened stress or anxiety which elevates tinnitus levels. Speaking out will help to relieve these issues and perhaps prevent a tinnitus outburst. Don't be afraid to speak up or change something that helps your tinnitus. There is no reason to be timid about doing this because it concerns your health. The benefit of educating others is to keep an emotional balance of wellbeing when engaging in the environment. Your attitude in adjusting to environments where tinnitus flare ups can occur will definitely teach non-sufferers the disruptive nature of tinnitus, thereby increasing awareness and support. Remember, if you don't take action and let tinnitus reign over internal feelings, stress and anxiety remains in your environment. The least amount control tinnitus has over emotions, the more of a reign you have. As you become more confident in taking action with skills in retraining the behavior of tinnitus, equilibrium should follow meaning less critical flare ups. This is success.

C = Conquer – Challenge

Conquering any change of attitude is a challenge. To conquer and challenge a negative tinnitus attitude is to become positively engaged in developing skills that assist in the ongoing battle in tinnitus control. To win this battle you need to lay claim to your life and how tinnitus has changed it by the way you have been thinking and acting towards having it. You can challenge these changes with your determination in discovering which coping skills work best at these tinnitus problems. Note that some skills may work better than others in defeating tinnitus problems. Whatever coping skills practiced consistently will improve control over tinnitus. The quicker you learn how to distract and redirect tinnitus the easier it becomes dealing with it. Doing something constructive with the mind, like focusing on a thought, a place, words or quotes, redirects and commands the obsessive sounds of tinnitus to change direction, level or disappears. This activity is found in the P.E.A.C.E. step. By taking action with words you distract and curb the control tinnitus has, lessening its' powerful influence over you. The brains' power gains more control. Having this increased control eventually helps to stop the brain from being pulled in a negative direction in listening to the magnetic sound that draws your focus and concentration away from whatever you're engaged in doing. Distracting the attention tinnitus sounds demand on your listening ear will bring about an increased sense of inner control.

Suggestions in conquering

There are other suggestions that complement the P.E.A.C.E. step that you might take into consideration when trying to defeat the tinnitus storms. Masking tinnitus, habituation, biofeedback, tinnitus retraining therapy, ear plugs or relaxation techniques such as yoga and meditation can be teamed together in learning how to control and conquer tinnitus noise. The use of multiple coping skills brings success quicker in lowering or silencing tinnitus. Since tinnitus can be an ongoing lifetime concern, the more coping skills acquired will help you deal with the nuisances.

E = Enjoyment

All people have the need for peace and joy. Unfortunately when stricken with tinnitus, this peace and joy seems to diminish. The trials and tribulations of tinnitus interferes with the peace and joy, replacing it with unwanted annoying sounds. As you continue to learn how to utilize techniques and conquer tinnitus, peace and joy returns as like an embrace. Again, how you adapt to it is by taking necessary measures to become in charge of the hearing disorder. Controlling the noise with skills brings an increase sense of interior peace. By engaging in favorable activities which also can be a coping skill, there is less focus on the disorder and brings about a sense of tinnitus silence. You may not even realize it when this silence occurs because it may be least expected.

Since enjoyment is from doing what makes you happy, any activity enjoyed alters tinnitus power. The mind is preoccupied and engaged positively elsewhere not giving into the attention tinnitus seeks. When you replace the negative focus on tinnitus by engaging in a positive focused activity only favorable results show up. A sense of wellbeing occurs. Remember tinnitus is a thief of peace and happiness. Let the P.E.A.C.E. step help you bring enjoyment back to life.

8

TACKLING A
STORM WITHIN

How do you tackle a tinnitus storm of noise within? By utilizing the P.E.A.C.E step in challenging your ability to defeat inner ear noise. Whether the noise is present daily or not, the main goal here is to remain in constant control of the inner ear noise at all times. To prevent tinnitus from taking back control and influence your life negatively, one must stop it quickly at the moment it flares up. Your inborn brain power has to learn how to defeat tinnitus brain power. The power in concentrating on quotes or words reclaims the direction of tinnitus power to control, slowly extinguishing its' noise down to a manageable level. The frequency of tinnitus interruptions becomes easier to manage. As tinnitus brews, the P.E.A.C.E. step helps you to remain calm, focused and in control.

In learning this P.E.A.C.E. step it will not only confront the control over your tinnitus, it will also ease symptoms like anxiety, depression, and irritability. Repeating words positively influences the negative effects of the ever changing tinnitus. By mentally practicing the P.E.A.C.E step it tackles the control tinnitus has by distracting the mesmerizing sound listened to. As the tinnitus noise level increases so does anxiety. When you speak out loud and listen to your voice repeating a P.E.A.C.E. word, the focus on tinnitus inner ear sound diminishes. Concentration and focus improves greatly, anxiety is reduced thereby you are in control. The effectiveness of word repetition can sometimes immediately stop the active tinnitus. Repetition is re-teaching the brain not to listen to the sounds. Word distraction can break the tinnitus repetitiveness of sound as well as its' level of loudness.

Word distraction is known to be a method for change in the Sanskrit language for centuries. It is believed in this classical language that when you say a word out loud it lifts to the sky towards a desire for change. When practicing the P.E.A.C.E. step by repeatedly saying or thinking inspirational positive words and quotes it can only bring positively change in controlling tinnitus. I suggest you write down the P.E.A.C.E. word or quote on a piece of paper and tape it up in areas where you see the words often. When tinnitus flares up, go to the area of the note and start repeating the word or quote numerous times until the tinnitus lessens. Remember be sincere with this intent. Writing or speaking words is an implementation in distracting the influential sounds of tinnitus. It helps to focus and calm you down.

Another way to let this coping skill of word distraction (P.E.A.C.E.) to work is to allow it to resonate in your body, mind and spirit by the use of breath. As you inhale with each breath say a word or quote. Hear the words in your mind and allow it to change the focus on tinnitus activity. Each breath holds the power to release tinnitus and make it still in evolving. Each breath of words holds the control over tinnitus. The more you focus with each breath of words, the easier it is to change the direction of your power over it. Consciously concentrate deeply and push the noise away in each breath. Let the pain depart and let the words replace the pain. For example, as you breathe in say the word peace, and as you exhale out say the word silence. Do this a few times until you notice a change in tinnitus level. Or perhaps say repetitively "Silence in, tinnitus out. Silence in, tinnitus out. Silence in, tinnitus out. It is only temporary, it is quiet. It is only temporary, it is quiet." This may still the activity of tinnitus irritation.

Remember the only way to quiet the storm within is that you become what tinnitus is good at and that is distraction and control. You need to become the distraction to tinnitus and take back the control tinnitus robs you of. Let words and quotes busy the tinnitus presence. Changing the dynamics in your control of tinnitus makes you the master of it. Let the P.E.A.C.E. step be your inspiration in resolving conflicts of tinnitus storms.

WORDS AND QUOTES
FOR P.E.A.C.E.

P – Power words

Power – Positive – Courage – Strength – Empowerment – Willpower –Belief – Dictator

Power belongs to those willing to dictate the positive course over the negative tinnitus control. All tinnitus sufferers have an innate ability to subdue their tinnitus problem.

Persistence – Perseverance – Will – Determination

Continue success by utilizing coping skills to gain total control over tinnitus.

Inspirational quotes for P

Power

"Put yourself in a state of mind where you say to yourself, here's an opportunity for me to celebrate like never before, my own power, and my own ability to get myself to do whatever is necessary." Tony Robbins

"The creation of a thousand forests is in one acorn." Ralph Waldo Emerson

"The miracle, or the power, that elevates the few is to be found in their industry, application, and perseverance under the promptings of a brave, determined spirit." Mark Twain

Determination

"Life is like a game of cards. The hand that is dealt you represents determinism; the way you play it is free will." Jawaharlal Nehru

"People of mediocre ability sometimes achieve outstanding success because they don't know when to quit. Most men succeed because they are determined to." George Allen

Perseverance

"By perseverance the snail reached the ark." Charles Haddon Spurgeon.

"Be like a postage stamp. Stick to it until you get there." Harvey Mackay. Harvey syndicated column. Mackay's United Features

Will

"Some say knowledge is power, but that is not true. Character is power." Sri Sathya Sai Baba

"Strength does not come from physical capacity. It comes from an indomitable will." Mahatma Gandhi

Willpower

"Willpower is the key to success. Successful people strive no matter what they feel by applying their will to overcome apathy, doubt or fear." Dan Milkman

"Willpower is a concentration of force. You gather up all your energy and make a massive thrust forward. Willpower is your ability to set a course of action and say, "Engage!" Willpower is the spearhead of self-discipline." Steve Palin

Belief

"If I have the belief that I can do it, I shall surely acquire the capacity to do it even if I may not have it at the beginning." Mahatma Gandhi

"If you believe you can, you probably can. If you believe you won't, you most assuredly won't. Belief is the ignition switch that gets you off the launching pad." Denis Whitley

"Being scared… We are to learn about fear, not how to escape it." Jidda Krishnamurti

Persistence

"Energy and persistence conquer all things." Benjamin Franklin 1706-1790

"Persistence work triumphs." Virgil

"The difference between try and triumph is just a little ump!" Marvin Phillips

E – Embrace words

Embrace – Accept – Acknowledge – Endurance

Embracing requires you to accept and acknowledge tinnitus difficulties and the noise it produces. Endurance is your persistence and strength to tolerate and deal with the interruptions of tinnitus noise in life.

Inspirational quotes for E

<u>Embrace</u>

"The remarkable thing is, we have a choice everyday regarding the attitude we will embrace for that day." Charles R. Swindle (American writer/clergyman)

"We must embrace pain and burn it as fuel for our journey." Kenji Miyazawa

"But pain...seems to me an insufficient reason not to embrace life. Being dead is quite painless. Pain, like time, is going to come on regardless. Question is, what glorious moments can you win from life in addition to the pain?" Lois McMaster Bujold

"Don't fear change, embrace it." Anthony J. D'Angelo (founder of Collegiate Empowerment and creator of Inspiration Books)

<u>Accept</u>

"The most important single ingredient in the formula for success is knowing how to get along with people. Theodore Roosevelt

"And the day came, when the risk to remain tight in a bud was more painful than the risk it took to blossom." Anais Nin

Acknowledgement

"I discovered early that the hardest thing to overcome is not a physical disability but the mental condition which it induces. The world, I found, has a way of taking a man pretty much at his own rating. If he permits his loss to make him embarrassed and apologetic, he will draw embarrassment from others. But if he gains his own respect, the respect of those around him comes easily." Alexander de Seversky

Endurance

"Some days are for living. Others are for getting through." Malcolm S. Forbes

"We all at certain times in our lives find ourselves broken. True strength is found in picking up the pieces." Jill Pendley

"Endurance is one of the most difficult disciplines, but it is to the one who endures that the final victory comes." Hindu Prince Gautama Siddhartha, 563-483 BC

"The first virtue in a soldier is endurance of fatigue; courage is only the second virtue." Napoleon Bonaparte, French Emperor 17th century

"Endurance is patience concentrated." Thomas Carlyle - Scottish Historian (1795-1881)

A – Action words

Action – Change – Adjust – Responsible – Ability

Being responsible by taking action to change the ability to handle and redirect the nature of tinnitus.

Allowance – Alter – Transform

A tinnitus sufferer must be able to make the allowance to alter and transform the toxicity of tinnitus.

Inspirational quotes for A

<u>Action</u>

"The future depends on what we do in the present." Mahatma Ghandi

"One of the most difficult things everyone has to learn is that for your entire life you must keep fighting and adjusting if you hope to survive. No matter who you are or what your position is, you must keep fighting for whatever it is you desire to achieve." George Allen (American football coach 1922-1990)

"I can't is a self-destructive and defeating statement, and does not energize action. It defeats the responsibility of the will. Saying "I can" empowers action of the will within. It takes a spirited courage to follow through with action." Elizabeth Kobe

Change

"Change your thoughts and you can change your world." Norman Vincent Peale

"There is no point in trying to change the world. It is incapable of change because it is merely an effect. Change your thought about the world. Here you are changing the cause. The effect will change automatically." D.T. Munda

"Attitudes are the means by which the creative mind trains the emotions. Attitudes are consciously chosen." D. T. Munda.

"Not everything that is faced can be changed, but nothing can be changed until it is faced." James Baldwin

"Nothing is predestined: the obstacles of your past can become the gateways that lead to the new beginnings." Ralph Blum

Adjusting

"When it is obvious that the goals cannot be reached, don't adjust the goals, adjust the action steps." Confucius (551-479)

"There are things I can't force. I must adjust. There are times when the greatest change needed is a change of my viewpoint." Denis Diderot – French Philosopher

"The meeting of two personalities is like the contact of two chemical substances: if there is any reaction, both are transformed." Carl G. Jung

"The only disability is a bad attitude." Scott Hamilton

"We cannot direct the wind, but we can adjust the sails." Dolly Parton – Singer

Responsibility

"Responsibility walks hand in hand with capacity and power." Josiah Gilbert Holland

"To see what is right and not to do it is to lack courage or principle." Confucius

"The pessimist complains about the wind, the optimist expects it to change, the realist adjusts the sails." William Arthur Ward

"Each handicap is like a hurdle in a steeplechase, and when you ride up it, if you throw your heart over, the horse will go along, too." Lawrence Bixby

C – Conquer words

Conquer – Triumph – Master – Defeat – Courage – Challenge – Control

To conquer and overcome tinnitus is having the skills and belief in gaining total control over it at any present time of its' interfering nature. Defeat tinnitus and become the master over it.

Inspirational quotes for C

<u>Conquer</u>

"When face with a mountain, I will not quit! I will keep on striving until I climb over, find a pass through, tunnel underneath, or simply stay and turn the mountain into a gold mine, with God's help." Dr. Robert H. Schuller

"You can never conquer the mountain. You can only conquer yourself." James Whittaker

"In any project the important factor is your belief. Without belief there can be no successful outcome." William James

Challenge

"There is no challenge more challenging than the challenge to improve you." Michael F. Staley

"Nothing is predestined: the obstacles of your past can become the gateways that lead to the new beginnings." Ralph Blum

"Life's challenges are not supposed to paralyze you; they are supposed to help you discover who you are." Bernice Johnson Reagon

"Difficulties are meant to rouse, not discourage. The human spirit is to grow strong by conflict." William Ellery Channing

Courage

"Courage is grace under pressure." Ernest Hemingway

"The future depends on what we do in the present." Mahatma Gandhi

"I want to do it because I want to do it." Amelia Earhart

"Have patience with all things, but chiefly have patience with yourself. Do not lose courage in conserving your imperfections, but instantly set about remedying them, every day begins the task anew." St. Francis de Sales

"A sense of humor is the pole that adds balance to our steps as we walk the tightrope of life." Arabian Proverb

Defeat

"Defeat is simply a signal to press onward." Helen Keller

"Every beginning is a consequence. Every beginning ends something." Paul Valery

Triumph

"Man needs his difficulties because they are necessary to enjoy success." Abdul Kalam

"If you can't excel with talent, triumph with effort." Dave Weinbaum

"Never underestimate your problem or your ability to deal with it." Robert H. Schuller

"Although there may be tragedy in your life, there is always a possibility to triumph. It does not matter who you are or where you come from. The ability to triumph begins with you." Oprah Winfrey

E – Enjoyment words

Enjoy – love – delight – pleasure – appreciate

In the crucial part of the tinnitus world, the sufferer always seeks to return to a prior level of joy, peace and happiness. With encouragement of thoughts here, no matter how tinnitus interrupts life, the key thing to remember is to keep your joy alive no matter how much work and effort is needed to rebuild and regain a sense of wellbeing and balance. The burden of having tinnitus can dissolve inner ear peace but you don't have to let it dissolve personal peace. Take the responsibility in finding a resolution to work with the tinnitus disorder and regain the joys of life.

Each day make a resolution to change tinnitus to create a healthier you. Implement P.E.A.C.E. in your activities and bring back the interior peace lost. Take a few minutes each day, practice P.E.A.C.E. and win over the influence tinnitus has on you. Remember it is the power in you and attitude that changes the nature of tinnitus control.

Inspirational quotes to Enjoy

"If the phone doesn't ring, it's me!" Jimmy Buffet – singer songwriter

"There are only two ways to live life. One is as though nothing is a miracle. The other is as if everything is." Albert Einstein

"All animals, except man, know that the principal business of life is to enjoy it." Samuel Butler

"The art of life is to know how to enjoy a little and to endure very much." William Hazlitt

"Know the true value of time; snatch, seize and enjoy every moment of it. No idleness, no laziness, and no procrastination: never put off till tomorrow what you can do today." Lord Chesterfield

"Start every day with a smile and get over with it." W. C. Fields

"It is time to come to your senses. You are to live and learn to laugh. You are to learn to listen to the cursed music of life and to reverence to the spirit behind it and to laugh at its distortions. So there you are. More will not be asked of you." Herman Hesse

"Laughter is a tranquilizer with no side effects." Arnold Glasow

"The human spirit needs to accomplish, to achieve, and to triumph to be happy." Ben Stein

"He that fears not the future may enjoy the present." Thomas Fuller

"Enjoy success that you have, and don't be hard on yourself when you don't do well. Too many times we beat up on ourselves. Just relax and enjoy it." Patty Sheehan

"The most important thing is to enjoy your life – to be happy – it's all that matters." Audrey Hepburn

"The way I see it, if you want the rainbow, you got to put up with the rain." Dolly Parton

About the Author

Elizabeth Marie Kobe is a nurse with over 20 years of professional medical experience. Her expertise spans from hospital to clinical to private client settings primarily in behavioral health. In 2004 she was involved in a target shooting incident where a gun was discharged very close to one of her ears. Upon suffering from incessant ringing sounds, hearing loss and sensation, she realized, "I have Tinnitus!" Deeply empathizing and understanding this great affliction in a very personal way, she has become very dedicated to helping guide the people that look to her for help.

Since that time the author has been actively working with Tinnitus sufferers by facilitating support groups, handling crisis intervention calls from all over the United States providing information and specialist locations. Conducts individual tinnitus support sessions, and lectures about preventing and managing tinnitus. She believes in going the extra mile to help distressed sufferers learn how to cope. She completely understands tinnitus and its affects and her efforts in helping others make a huge difference in their world.

Elizabeth is an avid hiker, hiking numerous miles on trails in New York, New Jersey, New England, Adirondacks and the Appalachian Trails. She enjoys poetry, archery, basketball, cross country skiing, ice skating, sewing, Early American history and an avid collector of antique cordial glassware dating back to 1800's. Lives on the east coast with family and a cat named "Alfred".